Muhammed Abed Mazeel

Restructuring and Re-organization of the Iraqi Oil Ministry and State-owned Oil Companies for Maximum Economic Growth and National Development

disserta
Verlag

Mazeel, Muhammed Abed: Restructuring and Re-organization of the Iraqi Oil Ministry and State-owned Oil Companies for Maximum Economic Growth and National Development, Hamburg, disserta Verlag, 2012

ISBN: 978-3-95425-004-2
Druck: disserta Verlag, Hamburg, 2012

Bibliografische Information der Deutschen Nationalbibliothek
Die Deutsche Nationalbibliothek verzeichnet diese Publikation in der Deutschen Nationalbibliografie; detaillierte bibliografische Daten sind im Internet über http://dnb.d-nb.de abrufbar.

Die digitale Ausgabe (eBook-Ausgabe) dieses Titels trägt die ISBN 978-3-95425-005-9 und kann über den Handel oder den Verlag bezogen werden.

© disserta Verlag, ein Imprint der Diplomica Verlag GmbH
http://www.disserta-verlag.de, Hamburg 2012
Hergestellt in Deutschland

Table of Contents

The revenue from this book will be donated to the sick cancer children and help organizations.

Dr Muhammed Abed Mazeel,

29.01.2012

About the Book

This book summarizes the recommendations for the re-structuring and re-organization of the oil industry in Iraq. My focus here is to use the restructuring and reorganization experience from national and international oil companies and to apply them to the Iraqi oil industry.

The Iraq Federal Administration should ensure a pragmatic approach to their current policy objectives. The current or future government needs to put into operation new policy instruments to facilitate oil and gas sector institutional restructuring.

Iraq should endeavor to produce its recoverable petroleum reserves optimally. The current administration must choose whether to allow the population to use the entire petroleum wealth derived from current petroleum production for their benefit or give future generations a share of the derived wealth from oil and gas development.

Introduction

The public mostly thinks that countries are happy and also lucky to have oil and gas reserves, truly these countries can base their economical development on these recoverable reserves (RR). The benefits of the economic growth are, increase government revenues to finance destitution facilitation, creation of jobs opportunities, improvement of infrastructure and support the private basic industry, agriculture, health system and basic food needs. But the experience of Iraq as oil exporting country to date illustrates very few of these benefits. To the contrary, the consequences of oil and gas production development tend to be negative, starting from dictator regimes which used the oil revenue to make three biggest wars after the II world war including slower than expected growth, barriers to economic diversification, poor social care performance, and high levels of destitution, inequality and unemployment. Iraq political change in 2003 characterized by exceptionally poor governance and high corruption, a culture of rent-seeking, often devastating economic, health and environmental consequences at the local level, and high occurrence of conflict and war /1/.

The Iraq social consequences generated by hydrocarbon dependence are; the type of pre-existing political, social and economic institutions available to manage oil wealth as it comes on-stream and, the extent to which oil revenues subsequently transform these institutions in a rentier direction. Iraq less-developed country where administrative institutions are weak, the cultural and social levels mainly delayed where religion and tradition plays main roll. Iraq needs essential reforms in the state political and civil structure, institutions and companies. Any meaningful reform in the oil and gas sector should include the reworking of existing policies, restructuring and reorganization of oil companies and the Ministry as well as the legal and regulatory framework and commercialization. It is important to provide the institutional framework that governs the operations of the industry, including the functions, powers, structures and funding of these institutions. The legislation in the upstream and downstream sectors focuses especially on matters of licensing, leases and contracts. The needs of the downstream natural gas include both technical and commercial licensing regulations and conditions. The legislation is essentially an amendment to the existing Technical Service Contracts (TSC) in Iraq and Production Sharing Contracts Agreements (PSC) in Iraqi Kurdistan based on the need to create a new fiscal framework that takes into consideration various compelling issues. The operations in the upstream of the industry include Licenses, leases and contracts /2/.

The restructuring would involve the shift from a domestic-based to a national and international business sector-based structure, the addition of many thousands corporate positions, to coin much of headquarters national and internationally, and the redesign of its systems of coordination and control. The restructuring would have been precipitated by the realization that Iraqi oil industry needed to change the way it did if it wanted to maintain the position of its state run chemical and energy industry and offer an adequate return to the public and indirectly to the shareholders of international partners in an increasingly turbulent industry environment.

From similar international companies and regional situations, it is clear that these changes would bring clear and defined benefits were bearing benefits. Costs would be optimized and the increase coordination and control that the new sector-based organisation permitted should help oil national companies to control costs, focus capital expenditure, and prune the business portfolio. The national oil company should consider the return on capital employed (ROCE) and return on equity (ROE) and not working as a socio-economic companies. Currently the Iraqi government used the oil revenue to pay a salaries and small inefficient infrastructure projects. However, much of the improvement in bottom-line performance was the result of the recovery in oil prices during the last years. Once the benefits of higher oil prices were stripped out, Iraq's improvements in financial performance looked much more modest. At the same time, International oil companies (IOC's) and National oil companies (NOC)'s) were not standing still. State Companies like, Saudi-Aramco, ADNOC, SONTRACH, OPDO, IRAN Oil Companies, and international oil companies like BP, Shell, Exxon-Mobile etc. had become one of the world's most dynamic, profitable, and widely admired oil majors. Its merger of many companies, in the meantime, Iraq oil companies was no longer a one of the world's oil producer leader– its sales revenues lagged some way behind some of oil majors. Other oil and gas majors were also getting caught up in the wave of mergers and restructurings. The merger of Total, Fina, and Elf Aquitaine in September 1999 had created the world's fourth "super-major" (after Exxon Mobil, Shell, and BP Amoco). Also asserting itself on the world stage was Italy's privatized and revitalized ENI S.p.A /3/.

The Iraq should take serious step in transformation the organizational structure of the oil institutions and companies. From a centralized confederation of many operating companies spread throughout the country under the leadership of the oil ministry, operation companies and divisionalized groups with clear lines of authority and more effective executive leadership would be create. Yet, Iraq oil ministry remained a highly complex organization that was a prisoner of its own illustrious history and where corporate authority re-mained in the ministry of oil. The main objective of the policies is to make far reaching changes and ensure the fundamental transformation of Iraqi Oil and Gas industry in order to optimize the development of the oil and gas industry; this in turn will hopefully maximize economic growth and overall country development. The develop-ment of the Iraqi oil and gas policies should be approved by the intended federal executive council under the chairmanship of the Minister President.

Summary

The first steps toward restructuring and reorganizing the institutions and the legislation include taking ownership of oil and gas resources, allocating acreages to Kurdistan/Iraq and neighbours states, Government participation, fiscal principles, and improving of transparency and good governance.

It is important to provide the institutional framework that governs the operations of the industry, including the functions, powers, structures and funding of these institutions.

The operations in the upstream of the industry include Licenses, leases and contracts. Other considerations covered are award processes, right of participation by the government, marginal fields, indigenous companies, termination and revocation of licenses and leases, matters on fees, rents and royalties and finally provisions on Associated Natural Gas.

The legislation in the downstream sector focuses especially on matters of licensing, refining and marketing of oil products, the transport logistics company, facility management companies, pipelines and depots and issues relating to pricing of products. The operating stocks and Iraq strategic stocks are also necessary.

The needs of the downstream natural gas include both technical and commercial licensing regulations and conditions, the network, gas supply licenses, transportation pipelines licenses and the whole sale market in addition to the possibility of third party access, customer protection, the pricing regime, and issues of public service obligations, competition and market regulation.

The legislation is essentially an amendment to the existing Technical Service Contracts (TSC) in Iraq and Production Sharing Contracts Agreements (PSC) in Iraqi Kurdistan based on the need to create a new fiscal framework that takes into consideration various compelling issues. The issues include the need to capture the full gas value chain for taxation purposes, developing a fiscal regime for gas that is removed from oil thereby creating a level playing field for all investors in gas, and promoting the effective management of costs across the industry –which in turn will maximize the government's take. Other considerations revolve around the requirement to develop a fiscal system that is responsive to the significant changes in prices; the need to clarify inconsistencies and/or conflicts in the application of fiscal terms for oil and gas; and finally, to develop a fiscal rule of general application based on a body of expected fiscal laws.

Quality, health, safety and environment are missing elements in Iraq. During the restructuring and reorganization of the institutions, the QHSE should take on a big role in working with the aforementioned departments in the Oil Ministry and the operating companies. The obligations of the state and international oil companies toward the state environmental regulations and public rules must be upheld according to the licensees, lessees and contractors with consideration for the matters of abandonment, decommissioning and disposal and their funding.

The various actors in the oil and gas production processes have obligations toward the various communities in the oil-producing region of the country. Supporting community development, providing employment opportunities, compensation, Infrastructure, protection and management of the environment are all essential components.

The Ministry of Oil remains essentially a civil service outfit that is ill-equipped to conceive and enact the required policies for such a complex and sophisticated industry. Therefore, there is a strong need for the principal and basic interaction between the following institutions:

- The Federal Oil Ministry
- Existing directorial and state oil companies
- Kurdistan Ministry of Energy and Natural Resources
- Private sector operatives

As well as the reorganization and restructuring of the following institutions:

- Federal Oil Ministry
- Existing directorial and state oil companies
- Iraqi National Oil Company and Iraqi National Gas Company

Regulatory Framework

Iraq has had a long history of oil exploration and development, and of foreign company investment, under both concession agreements and more recently through service contracts. In recent years, under the sanctions regime, production sharing contracts were negotiated and signed although none have been implemented to date.

Since Iraq ignore the presence of the Iraq National Oil Company (INOC), the Oil Ministry create own regulatory framework, it is dealing as a ministry and national oil company at the same time. The rules, polices, marketing and management are mixed together. Since Baghdad regime change in 2003, many unstudied rules are applied, starting from creating the general inspectorial office which is dealing in similar way to the criminal police office in the previous regime. The regulation allowed the ministry of oil to act as national oil company. It is heaved with unprofessional structure and Bureaucracy. Instead the Oil Ministry to start with reform of their structure and organization, it has since 2000, stated its preference for service-style contracts and introduced the DPC (Development and Production Contract) format as its preferred vehicle for future development projects. Under the Baath party regime, a fiscal and legislative framework for oil and gas production was long-established in Iraq as were the legal and tax systems. Signed petroleum contracts had the force of law. The regulatory structure of the Iraqi oil sector in the post-Saddam era is still evolving. Legislation governing the country's future hydrocarbon industry has recently been the subject of detailed political negotiations. In February 2007, the Council of Ministers reached agreement on a draft Federal Oil and Gas Law. Before entering into force, the legislation will need to be enacted by the Council of Representatives. The parliamentary vote was initially scheduled for end of May 2007, but by September 2008 the law had not been passed.

Nationalization

Historically, the early oil industry in Iraq was dominated by a single concession which had been granted to the Iraq Petroleum company (IPC - formerly known as the Turkish Petroleum Company) in 1925. The dominance of IPC was eroded following the Iraqi revolution in 1958. In 1961, the government promulgated Law No. 80, which was to be the first stage in the nationalisation of the oil industry. The law provided for the expropriation of the undeveloped areas of the company's concession and resulted in the IPC retaining 0.5 per cent of the area that had previously been held.

INOC

In February 1964, the Revolutionary Command Council enacted Law No. 97, establishing a state oil company known as the Iraq National Oil Company (INOC). The new organisation was sanctioned by the state to operate in all areas of the oil industry. At this time, however, the government did not possess the technical expertise and financial capability to take over the IPC's assets. Service contract agreements were concluded with a number of foreign oil companies including Elf, Braspetro and ONGC of India. At the same time, Iraq signed a technical agreement with the Soviet Union which paved the way for new-style 'working contracts'. Under the terms of these contracts the Soviet firms acted as operator and were remunerated regardless of their operational achievements.

Decree Law No. 69

In June 1972, the government promulgated Decree Law No. 69 under which all of IPC's assets and rights in Iraq were nationalised. The assets of IPC's two subsidiaries - Basrah Petroleum Company and Mosul Petroleum Company - were progressively nationalised over several years, with the process eventually being completed in December 1975.

Recent Development

Several significant events have taken place in Iraq which has critically affected the development of the country's upstream industry. These include:

- The Iran-Iraq war from 1980-88
- The Iraqi invasion of Kuwait in 1990 and the ensuing Gulf War conflict
- The years of under-investment and restrictions due to UN sanctions
- • The 2003 war and subsequent political instability

UN Sanction Regime

In response to Iraq's invasion of Kuwait in 1990, comprehensive economic sanctions were applied to Iraq, which prohibited the country from engaging in international trade. After the Gulf War ended, sanctions remained in force subject to Iraq's disarmament and cooperation with international weapons inspectors. However, under Resolution 986, the UN Security Council decided to allow Iraq to sell oil in return for essential civilian needs, such as food and medicine.

In May 1996, after extensive negotiations, a Memorandum of Understanding was signed between the Iraqi government and the United Nations to enable the sale of humanitarian goods in exchange for oil under the framework set out under Resolution 986. This established the terms of reference for what generally came to be referred to as the UN Oil-for-Food programme. The programme imposed a $2 billion ceiling on oil sales for each six-month phase. The ceiling was later raised to US$5.2 billion; although in reality the dilapidated state of Iraq's oil industry meant that the country's reduced production capacity had become the major limiting factor. In 1998, starting with Phase 4, Iraq was authorised to import up to $300 million (subsequently increased to US$600 million) worth of oil industry spare parts and equipment per phase.

Despite these modifications to the regime, sanctions had the effect of precluding almost all foreign investment in Iraq's oil and gas industry. During the 1990s, a number of companies sought to position themselves in Iraq for oil development opportunities once sanctions had been lifted. Yet those that had negotiated specific contracts (including LUKoil and CNPC) were not able to start work, although coming under considerable Iraqi pressure to do so.

More than $64 billion worth of oil was sold under the Oil-for-Food programme during a seven year period from 1996 to 2003. Economic sanctions were terminated in 2003 immediately after Saddam Hussein's removal from power in Iraq by a US-led military coalition. Under Security Council Resolution 1483, the administration of ongoing activities under the Oil-for-Food programme was initially transferred to the Coalition Provisional Authority before becoming the responsibility of the transitional Iraqi government in 2004.

2005 Constitution of Iraq

Iraq held landmark elections for a national assembly on the 30 January 2005, whose major task would be to draft a new constitution. As the Sunni groups had boycotted the elections, the constitution writing process was driven largely by a Shia-Kurdish alliance. The institutional framework that emerged was one centred upon the principles of federalism and decentralisation, whereby provinces and regions, such as Kurdistan in the north of Iraq, would have the right to form their own government and function with a high degree of autonomy.

With respect to questions of petroleum jurisdiction, only petroleum assets described as 'present' are dealt with explicitly in the constitution. Article 112 states that these assets are the responsibility of the federal government. Jurisdiction concerning fields that are not currently producing, i.e. those which have been discovered but not developed or have yet-to-be discovered, is merely implied by the operation of those articles that deal with the powers of both the federal government and regional governments, respectively.

Article 110 of the constitution, which lists the extent of the federal government's powers, omits the issue of petroleum jurisdiction completely. Article 115 then states that all powers not specified under Article 110 belong to regional authorities. It was on this basis that the Kurdistan Regional Government (KRG) argued that it had exclusive jurisdiction over petroleum exploration and development in Kurdistan with respect to non-currently producing fields. Controversially, this would have included all of Kurdistan's petroleum resources, as there were no fields being commercially produced in that part of Iraq when the constitution came into effect.

The Production Sharing Contracts awarded by the KRG since 2003 have not been recognized by the federal government and the question of the KRG's authority in this area has been an issue of contention. Efforts to resolve the dispute within the framework of a national hydrocarbons law were the subject of political negotiations in 2006 and 2007. This process led to the conclusion of a draft federal oil and gas law, which was endorsed by the Council of Ministers on 15 February 2007.

2007 Federal Oil and Gas Law

The principal objectives of the new law are threefold:

- To separate the regulated activities of production and oil services companies from the regulatory, monitoring, and supervisory departments in the Ministry of Oil

- To provide a framework that enables effective cooperation between federal and regional authorities

- To create an enabling environment for the market to play a major role in the development of Iraq's oil and gas resources.

The law defines a role for the Ministry of Oil that is primarily regulatory in character and which will not include any direct involvement in field operations. Petroleum development activities in Iraq will be undertaken by an independent Iraq National Oil Company and its subsidiaries as well as other commercial organizations. Achieving federal-regional cooperation will be the responsibility of a new 12-member body, named the Federal Oil and Gas Council (FOGC), whose primary function will be to ensure that all contracts granted by

Iraq's prescribed authorities meet both procedural and substantive criteria. An Independent Panel of Advisors will act as a panel of judges to safeguard the impartiality of any decision reached. The roles of the different bodies, and their relationship to one another, are summarized in the Regulatory Body section below.

Outstanding Issues

Agreement on the Federal Oil and Gas Law represents an important step forward in the future governance of Iraq's petroleum sector. To complete the process, however, a number of outstanding issues must be resolved, including the need for the law to be enacted by parliament.

The initial prospects of the law's passage appeared to be good, with a parliamentary deadline set for the end of May 2007. However, a political disagreement between the KRG and Oil Ministry, which surfaced in April 2007, has prevented any meaningful progress.

The process broke down over the question of how Iraq's oil and gas fields and exploration areas are to be allocated between the Designated Authorities. Other important issues have yet to be resolved, including the different model contracts that will form the guidelines against which future contracts will be judged, and a law governing the distribution of petroleum revenues from oil and gas development.

Regulatory Body

In 1976, the Iraqi oil industry was subject of a wholesale re-structuring and re-organisation. A new Ministry of Oil was established, with far-reaching powers over planning and construction in the petroleum sector with responsibility for oil refining, gas processing, and internal marketing of gas products through several subsidiary organizations. In 1987, further changes were introduced following the appointment of Issam al-Chalabi as Iraq's oil minister.

INOC was absorbed into the Ministry of Oil and the three existing state agencies responsible for refining; oil distribution and gas were converted into new departments of the Ministry. The regional entities within INOC were reduced from three to two, to form the North Oil Company and the South Oil Company. The assimilation of these state run companies further consolidated management of Iraq's oil production and distribution systems within the Ministry. Several other new organisations within the Oil Ministry were set up at this time, including the State Oil Marketing Organisation, Iraq Oil Exploration Company and separate oil and gas distribution companies.

Additional restructuring took place in 1998 and this subdivided the Oil Ministry into 22 separate organizations. Of these, six companies are included in the Upstream division, eight companies are included in the Downstream division, and nine are included within the Directorates division. These are listed as follows:

Upstream Division: North Oil Company, South Oil Company, Misan Oil Company, State Company for Oil Projects, Iraqi Drilling Company, Oil Exploration Company

Downstream Division: LPG Bottling Company, North Refining Company, Central Refinery Company, South Refining Company, North Gas Company, South Gas Company, Oil Products Distribution Company, Petroleum Pipeline Company

Directorates and Others: State Oil Marketing Company, Iraqi Tanker Company, National Manufacturing Department, Economics and Finance Department, Administration and Legal Department, Planning Studies and Follow-up Directorate, Technical Directorate, Reservoir and Fields Development Directorate, Control and Internal Audit Directorate.

New Institutional Framework

Throughout the recent period of political transition in Iraq, the Ministry of Oil has remained in control of the oil industry in Arab Iraq and the various state-run companies engaged in upstream and downstream operations. The structural make-up of the Ministry has remained the same, with key changes being the removal of the organisation's high-ranking political figures. However, the draft Federal Oil and Gas Law provides for a major transformation of the relationship between the Ministry of Oil, on the one hand, and the state operating companies, on the other.

State Oil Company

The Preamble of the 2007 Federal Oil and Gas Law affirms that oil activities operated solely by the Ministry of Oil will be transferred to technical and commercial entities and institutions, including an independent Iraq National Oil Company (INOC). INOC will be constituted as a financially and administratively independent organisation owned wholly by the Iraqi government. The law specifies that INOC will manage and operate Iraq's currently producing fields, as well as participate in the development of discovered fields which are not yet currently producing. These assets are to be listed in two of four annexes to the Law, which have still to be defined.

INOC will be a holding company within which existing state companies, particularly the North and South Oil Companies, will be subsumed. It will also own and operate the main pipeline network and export facilities in Iraq, as well as administer export licensing arrangements - a task that is currently performed by the State Oil Marketing Organisation. However, the law stipulates that control of the pipeline network is to be for a two year transitional period only, until the Ministry of Oil has been reorganized. In sum, INOC will take over all of the Ministry's major operating arms, including oil and gas exploration, development, production, transportation, storage, marketing and sales.

State Participation

State participation is a feature of both the production sharing contracts in Kurdistan and the technical service contracts (TSCs) awarded by the Ministry of Oil. The Kurdistan Regional Government has a participating interest in many of the licenses that it has awarded since 2004. The Iraqi TSCs all include a 25% state equity partner. A number of state-owned companies are involved. They include the major operating companies - North Oil, South Oil and Misan Oil-as well as several other agencies and organisations: the State Oil Marketing Organisation, the Iraqi Drilling Company and the Oil Exploration Company. Under the terms of the contract, the state partner can elect to have its costs carried by the other members of the consortia /44/.

Licensing

Due to the presence of UN sanctions, licensing in Iraq has been very limited since 1990. Sanctions did not explicitly preclude negotiations for development or exploration contracts and this led to several European and other non-US companies holding contract discussions and negotiations with the Iraqi Ministry. However, the sanctions prevented US and UK companies holding any such discussions with the Ministry and effectively stalled actual development activity on the contracts signed by the non-US parties. Significant new contract awards in non-Kurdish controlled areas, and implementation of existing contracts, are not expected until the Federal Oil and Gas Law has been passed and the security risk has reduced to acceptable levels.

In Kurdistan, the Ministry of Natural Resources is the organ which administers petroleum operations in Kurdish controlled territory. Legislation enacted by the KRG in 2007 stipulates that the Ministry is responsible for negotiating, agreeing and executing all contracts entered into by the KRG. The KRG's status as the prescribed licensing body in Kurdistan is confirmed in the draft federal legislation.

Contracts Award Process under the New Law

The Ministry of Oil, INOC and Regional Authorities are nominated as Designated Authorities (DA) under the 2007 draft regime, and hold the right to award contracts for conducting petroleum operations within assigned areas. An institutional process has been designed to satisfy the conflicting views of the KRG and federal government with respect to the former's degree of autonomy in the award of petroleum development contracts.

Once a contract has been granted, the DA must submit it to the Federal Oil and Gas Council (FOGC) within 30 days. The FOGC will approve the contract or refer it to the PIA, if it is considered to be inconsistent with FOGC guidelines. The decision of the PIA on the validity of the contracts must be communicated to the DA within 60 days. If it is ruled to be invalid, the contract must be amended and re-submitted according to the same process.

Oil Ministry Production Target and Market Requirements

According to the International Energy Agency's (IEA's) forecast, the call on OPEC crude oil production by 2020 will have increased by about 3mn b/d from the year 2008. The IEA estimate assumes a weak annual growth in oil demand and an increase in non-OPEC supply of 3mn b/d. By comparison, the CGES forecast estimates, by 2020, an increment of 6.5mn b/d on the call for OPEC oil, with the assumption of 1% global demand growth per annum, and an increase in non-OPEC supplies of 500,000 b/d /45/.

This would imply that, in the interests of maintaining a world market balance and not creating undue downward pressure on world oil prices, OPEC's incremental production in the coming 10 years should not exceed the range estimated by the IEA and CGES /4, 43, 45/.

However the timing and magnitude of the planned production expansion program coupled with world economic recession and the projected continuation of weak oil demand are expected to make hard for Iraq to achieve full potential within this decade. The intended revenue gains to Iraq are not anticipated to be realized in full within the planned time frame and would require greater efforts to make the most of a difficult situation. The delicate oil market balances lying ahead require extremely good judgment and policy applications.

Moreover Iraq oil transportation system, storage capacities, loading infrastructure and facilities are only adequate to cater for limited amounts of oil exports of around the 3 mbd or may be slightly higher. Plans to expand on these capacities although are considered vital for the proposed production program they are still very indicative and have yet to see some serious actions /4, 5, 6, 8, 9, 18, 19, 20/.

Further results are future conflict with the OPEC and the international oil companies this will influence the economy of Iraq in negative way. To serve Iraq's economy, the only way out for the Ministry of Oil is to curb its ambitious strategy, avoid its present chaos commitments to the oil companies, with the objective of reaching a more reasonable addition to its capacity.

The Revenue of the Own State Oil Companies Permit Cumulative Policy Errors

Disabled and unproductive governance, perhaps more than any other factor, may explain the extent of destitution in oil-dependent Iraq, but this too is related to heritage of the presence of oil. Because the revenue base of the state is the state, oil rents affect state capacity. Oil dependence warps the institutional development of the state because oil rents weaken factorships of constraint. In resource poor countries intense population pressure on scarce resources reduces the tolerance for inefficiency and predation, and the economy cannot support extensive protection or an over-expanded bureaucracy. But in oil states, the brake of scarcity does not exist. Instead, oil dependence encourages the expansion of states into new arenas while weakening opportunities to strengthen administrative capacities, especially non oil-based tax systems, merit-based civil services, and the rule of law – fundamental elements for creating efficient states /7, 8, 9/. Iraq oil rents impact on effective governance has a pernicious effect on the quality of administrative institutions, regardless of whether they are democratic or authoritarian. Since 1927 Iraq oil is the major steering for the economy, the state do not have to extract the majority of their resources from their own populations, they do not have to build the institutional capacities that have historically been required by such extraction. They do not have the urgent need for heritage change of the ministries and their companies, even though it is inefficient and ineffective way of working. This means that they are denied the incentives for innovation of reorganization and restructuring the existing companies and institutions and any a civil service that stems from austerity. In general, oil rents permit incapable state institutions to endure and poor policies persist to persist considerably longer than in less resource rich countries. To avoid unpopular reforms, governments use their oil as collateral for borrowing abroad or intensify the squeeze on the export sector. Petrodollars simply permit more scope for cumulative policy errors.

Existing Organization-Structuring of the Institutions and Companies Encourage the Corruption

Iraq as oil exporting country have the greatest resource endowments, also have extraordinarily high levels of corruption specially after the regime change in 2003– a reality confirmed by stunning quantitative evidence and numerous case studies. With incomes of the order $100-120 billion/year for Iraq, the temptations for abuse are immense, and with weak state capacity and rule of law in place, there is little institutional restraint. "People rob," Oil rents and institutional weakness form a vicious cycle. Quantitative evidence suggests that the extent of corruption is higher in Iraq in which civil service recruitment and promotion procedures rely less on merit-based considerations; where this is the case, efforts to reform the civil service are blocked in order to sustain patterns of corruption. At its worst, this can degenerate into a "corruption trap," where payoffs at the top of political and business institutions encourage the corruption of others until a large percentage of public and private sector figures are involved, as the case of Iraq demonstrates /10, 21, 22, 23, 24/.

Corruption takes place not only at the production and export stage through secret signature bonuses and opaque financial arrangements, but also as a result of extremely high and difficult to absorb investments at the "upstream" stage as well as at the trading or "downstream" stage, where massive resources tend to disappear through price transfers that are difficult to track. While transactions are obviously clandestine, evidence of oil-related corruption abounds in both the private sector and the state. The situation of state in state Kurdistan state in state of Iraq and the main Iraq political unstable situation, encourage the corruption contributes to the resource curse. Rulers will support existing organization and structuring of institutions and companies that produce personalized rents even if these policies result in lower overall social care and because they need to share these rents with supporters and subordinates, the level of distortion can be very great. Organization and structuring and generally policy choices are deformed in a number of ways. The corruption affects economic growth and income levels and reduces the quality of public services as well as lowering the quality of public infrastructure.

Social Consequences of Iraq Hydrocarbon Management

One of the most important social consequences of the Iraq resource management is that Iraq as oil-exporting country has high destitution rates, poor health centre, high rates of child mortality, and poor educational performance given their revenues. While it is true that most forms of primary commodity dependence are associated with destitution, not all commodities are equally culpable. Countries dependent on agricultural commodities tend to perform better with respect to destitution, minerals in general are linked to high levels of destitution, and oil dependence in particular is correlated with low life expectancy and high underfeeding rates.

Oil dependence has an ambiguous relationship with destitution facilitation, and this is related to the boom-crash cycles accompanying dependence on the resource. At the beginning of oil exploitation for export, per capita income rises during the "intoxication" or "boost" period. Especially in the initial stages of production for export, petroleum revenues initially transform a society-often suddenly and dramatically. Employment increases, infrastructure is improved, and per capita income grows rapidly. But the failure to diversify from oil dependence into other self-sustaining economic activities, especially agriculture and works-intensive industry, becomes a significant obstacle to pro-poor development /11, 12, 13, 25, 26, 27/.

For Iraq, this plunge has been very severe - moving real per capita incomes back to the 1970s and 1980s. After Kuwait invasion 1991, the USA and their alliance war and sanction against Iraq from 1991 to regime break-up in the third golf war in 2003, the growth of destitution has been dramatically increased; real per capita income has lead to 1940 levels. It is almost as if sixty years of development had not taken place.

The Rule Centralization Autocracy

Oil and centralized rule seem to go together; the conflict between Regional Government of Kurdistan and main Iraq central Government, and the function-ability of oil institutions and Iraq new democracy are mixed. Political scientists have repeatedly documented this relationship through case studies, and they have found a robust and statistically significant association between oil depend-ence and authoritarian government's /12/. Oil appears to constrict the appearance of democracy in most cases, Iraq exception became through break-up of Saddams regime through USA and their Alliance. The hindering of democratization seems to occur primarily through different, though related, process. The first is based on how reinter states collect revenues. Because Iraq live from oil rents rather than direct taxation, it is likely to tax their populations lightly or not at all. Thus, it is unusually detached from and unaccountable to the general population, and its population, in turn, is less likely to demand accountability from and representation in government. In effect, the vital link between taxation and representation is broken. Another factor depends on how Iraq regimes spend state revenues. Oil fortune produces greater spending on customer that, in turn, weakens existing pressures for representation and accountability. In effect, popular accordance is achieved through the political distribution of rents. Oil states can buy political agreement, and their access to rents facilitates the cooptation of potential disputant or dissident voices.

The work ethics are undermined and negative attitudes towards certain forms of work, especially manual works. This in turn can translate into lower levels of productivity than those found in comparable resource poor states. The Iraqi's with their sudden influx of income they did not work hard to get have not usually developed the fiscal and financial discipline or work habits normally required to get and keep such windfalls. The disparity created by oil-led development appear to be at about the same levels as non-oil states with similar incomes, people in oil-exporting countries may experience these disparity very differently because they occur in what is widely perceived to be a rich country /13, 14, 28, 29, 30/.

Oil Management Development

Oil management development means economic development can be accepted change in the structure of the economy. Structural change refers to terms such as agricultural transformation, industrialization, demographic transition, urbanization, transformation of domestic demand and production, foreign trade, finance, and employment. In considering structural changes is the pattern of the Iraq's economic growth and or shrank and to determine it's achieved level of development. One clear pattern of the changing economic structure in the course of economic development is that the share of industry increases as gross output per capita rises. The difference in the output and the contribution to GDP of the industrial sector in developing countries as opposed to its place in developed countries was seen as the main manifestation of economic backwardness and dependence. While value added growth rate in the Iraq oil sector was fluctuating during the period 1927–1991, the other sectors are decreasing in the war time and not adding significant value to the growth rate.

Strategy and Organizational Structural Changes of Oil Majors

The world petroleum industry was transformed by a number of fundamental changes. The growing power of the producer countries is dominated by state-owned companies such as Saudi Aramco, Petroleos de Venezuela, Kuwait Oil, Iran National Oil Company, Pemex (Mexico), and Russia's Gasprom and Lukoil. In addition, the old-established majors faced competition from other sources. The "new majors," integrated oil companies such as Elf, Aquitaine (France), Total (France), ENI (Italy), Nippon Oil (Japan), Neste (Finland), and Respol (Spain), were expanding rapidly, while in North America and the North Sea independent E&P companies such as Enterprise Oil, Triton, and Apache were becoming significant global players. Between 1985 and 1993, almost all the world's oil majors underwent far-reaching restructuring. Restructuring is involved radical simultaneous changes in strategy and organizational structure in a compressed time-frame. Key features of restructuring by the oil majors were /15, 16, 17, 18, 31, 32, 33/:

- Reorienting their goals around shareholder value maximization

- Greater selectivity in their strategies

- Cutting back on staff, especially at the corporate level.

- Reducing excess capacity through refinery closures and sales and scrapping of oceangoing tankers

- Decentralization of decision making from corporate to divisional levels and from divisional to business unit levels at the same time as giving divisions and business units full profit and loss responsibility

- Shifting the basis of organizational structure from geographical organization around countries and regions to worldwide product divisions (many of the majors formed worldwide divisions for upstream activities, downstream activities, and chemicals)

- Delivering through eliminating administrative layers within hierarchical structures

For example, Amoco broke up its three major divisions (upstream, downstream, and chemicals) and had 17 business groups reporting direct to the corporate centre. Mobil also broke up its divisional structure, and created 13 business groups.

Required Change Process

The minister president should take a step within oil institutions and companies, proponents of organizational change, including the heads of several of the operating, service and marketing companies, the administration and finance function, and directorate and divisions, had little success in the existing structure. The minister president should call for a meeting of oil institutions, companies, advisers, independent expertise and private sector. The request for frank discussions of the reasons for Iraq oil industry, development, structuring, organisation returns, investment nationally and internationally and public shares and revenue distribution. The outcome should the appointment of a high-level team to study Iraq's internal organization and come up with options for redesign. The internal team from the Iraqi oil industry and institutions should joined by seniors consultants from international market. The starting point for the internal team should a program of interviews with managers at different levels. This provided a basis both for assessing the existing structure and for generating ideas for change. The role of the consultants should to provide perspective, to challenge the ideas of the team, to introduce the experiences of other large multinationals, to provide the backup research needed to refine and test out ideas and concepts, and to organize the program of work and consultation. The team should prepare a diagnosis of the existing oil ministry and their own state companies' structure together with a suite of options for reorganization. It should illustration of through workshops, to explore in more details the specific dimensions of change and to clarify and evaluate the available options. The results of this exercise should identify the areas for change and the options. The team should identify the objects of change and how the different options related to these. The driving force behind the redesign is the desire to have a simpler structure in which the Iraq National Oil Company, Iraq National Gas Company and Oil Ministry relationships would be clearer and thus to allow the corporate centre to exert more effective influence and control over the operating companies. A simpler structure would help eliminate some of the cost and inertia of the oil ministry bureaucracies. There is also a need to improve coordination between the Operating companies rather than oil ministry. For example, in exploration and production, critical issues related to the development and application of new technologies and sharing of best practices. In downstream, the critical issues related to the rationalization of capacity, the pursuit of operational efficiency, and the promotion of the Iraqi Oil refineries, petrochemicals and other products brand. The final approval should come from the minister president and his advisers committee /19, 20, 33, 34/.

Re-organization and Reforms of Own State Oil Companies

The purpose of the reorganisation is to separate the functions of government and the enterprises and to break down the traditional upstream and downstream monopolies, or split system, by establishing multi enterprises competition, to promote momentum with the Iraqi oil industry by introduction of market principals and mechanism created by the establishment of this multi enterprise competitive system, to establish comprehensive petroleum enterprises like the major internationals in order to increase global competitiveness.

The business reorganisation and reforms, the traditional government functions should changed, allowing the national oil and gas companies to maintain autonomous management and separate government functions and business functions. It should be not under any new restructuring, direct participation in the management activities by means government orders and administrative directives. Under the new petroleum law and new polices of Iraq, the oil industry government administration could supervise and guide the oil industry and their business activities. As a result of simplified organisational structure, the function of oil industry's administrative system is mainly to guide and supervise the direction of the industry's management and production activities through laws and policies.

Separation of Government and Enterprise Improved Efficiency of Management and Production Organization

Under the new oil industry structure, direct participation in management activities as currently, by means of government orders and administrative directives could no longer occur. In additional as a result of government structure reforms and slimming down and improved efficiency in oil industry administrative structure structures, the government via state law and policies should be able to establish industry plans, development polices, strategies and technical standard, and to supervise and guide industry's activities.

Vertically Integrated Industry

The INOC should focus on the oil and gas development, while the same time could carried out work in downstream areas such refinery and marketing. Beside that the oil ministry should create new groups from the reorganisation and reforms continue to inter-enterprise competition, while aiming to improve international competitiveness, and realize economic growth. As a result of the planed reorganisation and reforms, is the separation between the main and alongside businesses, namely stripping away non-profitable section from profitable section and creating limited companies in a bid to improve efficiency in management and production. Over plus employees could be transferred to other new created companies. If the plan is to bring the companies in the stock market, then a cost cutting move is necessary. A simplified the organisation of the INOC and focusing on exploration, production and marketing. Furthermore in carrying out the separation in main businesses and auxiliary businesses, reorganisation and reforms, also transfer the groups non profitable alongside businesses sections, such as schools, security structure and other possible units to the government. Refining operations reforms is to promote and the intermediate department layers should divided and or merge with other posts. Furthermore reforms and reorganisations with the marketing system are required. For example oil products distribution company (OPDC) head quarter, regional marketing (OPDC), provincial marketing (OPDC), city marketing company (OPDC) could simplify and new accounting company responsible for their accounting activities /36, 37/.

The Significance of Overseas Stock Market Listing

Under the reforms and organisations, the government needs to attract the investors, to direct the oil ministry increasing structural reforms and to pursue listings oil companies in overseas stock markets. So that Iraq can realize funds from majors oil companies and international shares holders, for example in the refining sector, INOC could be able to a strategic alliance with oil majors. The INOC could made use of the partner technology and funds to plan oil refinery expansions. Furthermore for better economic resources is very important to develop the petrochemical projects. This will implement effective investment expansion which Iraq need to cover the shortage in the budget, the same time cover the shortage in crude oil products for the domestic market and export for the international market /21, 38, 39/.

Iraq oil industry needs to progress in strategic tie-ups with international majors with the goal of the capitalizing on their branding and marketing expertise. The oil products marketing company or in today in Iraq oil products distribution company needs jointly establish company with oil majors to operate in and outside the country.

The principal factor of success is strong domestic management and production, overseas advancement and confidence, the rationalization of the production organization through reductions in surplus manpower improve business and production efficiency, the company profile correspond to international market competitions using the international practices and rules, including information disclosure systems and international accounting standards /22, 40, 41/.

Business Strategy of the Proposed Iraq Oil Companies

- **Business Strategies**

Utilizing the existing oil and gas fields and expanding it is upstream production. At the same time the company needs to move to make advancement in profitable sectors like refining and petrochemicals. In additional the company further expansion to provide LNG and natural gas electrical generation.

- **Overseas Exploration and Development Activities**

The needs for development overseas projects with the characteristics of their business resources, Exploration, development and production as well the downstream projects. The need of globalization of their business is an important economic strategy.

Government/Business Relationship

The appointment and dismissal of top company's personnel should be proposed by federal oil and gas consul (FOGC), International Consulting Adviser, and ultimately decide after screening by the parliament preventatives. These are the chiefs of the enterprises, as well as government top officials (equivalent to minister position) but are high qualified technocrats.

Characteristics of Human Network Relationships

The companies should have human network relationship and a route for connection to the minister president and parliaments. Through these communications firms can report to the government members. The oil firms can benefit greatly from involvement high ranking government officials in case of screening permission of large scale projects such as construction of new refineries and or overseas investment, as the visit of these bureaucrats to the country of the proposed project can speed the process along.

Governments Stockholding

Through state-run parent companies and state run banks, the Iraqi government wills controls the oil companies planned listed in the stock markets. The government stock holder ratio should be very high in order to have a great degree of influence over the organization,

important personnel, asset and decisions and production.

Government Policy/Command Participation

The government not only instructs the state oil firms to increase production and profits in terms of business, it is also continually instructs and guides the companies leadership through administrative means and parliaments to ensure the stable development. In consideration of the company stability, the top leadership of the companies would be informed by the government of flexibility options that should be adopted, where possible-in the form of voluntary redundancies, temporary layoffs and transfers to suitable external posts, so that the organisational reforms and restructuring could be best implemented.

Preferential Treatment in Terms of Government Policies and Financing

The oil companies with their huge revenue to the country, the government should have the regards and project flexibility permissions and providing preferable financing measures, such as lowering interest rate for loans.

Supporting Resources Diplomacy

Usually the diplomacy often led to the aforementioned exploration and development agreements that allowed acquiring overseas oil field rights and investments.

The New Structure

The business organizations should created to achieve closer integration within each business sector across the country. The aim of the new structure would allow more effective planning and control within each of the businesses, remove much of the top-heavy bureaucracy that had imposed a costly burden on the companies, and eliminate the power of the regional fiefdoms. The new structure would strengthen the executive authority of the Committee of Managing Directors by providing a clearer line of command to the business organizations and subsequently to the operating companies, and by splitting central staff functions into a Corporate Centre and a Professional Services Organization. The existing is not similar to structure in the world; the proposed new one would produce professional services to companies with ministry of oil and the group of companies. The organizational structure should consider the following /23, 42/:

- The decentralized structure based on the autonomy of the INOC operating companies
- The new structure continued the distinction between governance and executive responsibility

The Existing Structure

It is important to consider the existing structure and policies. The principal changes in the existing structure are the changes involving the identities and roles of operation and the service companies to create a closer alignment with the new management structure.

Required Change Process

- **The Management Structure**

The proposed organizational structure describes in terms of the organizational elements the business organizations, the corporate centre, professional services, the operating units, the operating companies and the committee of managing director's /24/.

- **The Business Organizations**

The central feature of the new organization structure is the new Business Organizations. The Committee Managing Directors are supported by the Business Organizations: Exploration and Production ("upstream"), oil products ("downstream"), chemicals, and gas. The Business Organizations should headed by Business Committees made up of a number of Business Directors appointed by the Committee Managing Directors. These Business Directors included /24, 25, 26, 43/:

- Business Directors with responsibility for particular business segments

- Certain of the operating companies is so important that their Chief Executives should be Business Directors

- A Business Director for Research and Technical Services

- A Business Director for Strategy and Business Services

- The Business Committees are responsible and accountable to Committee Managing Directors for:

- the strategy of their business area;

    • endorsing the capital expenditure and financial plans of the operating companies and business segments within their business area;

    • appraising operating company and business segment performance; and

    • availability of technical, functional, and business services to the operating companies within their business sector.

Chairing each of the Business Committees is a member of the Committee Managing Directors.

- **The Corporate Centre**

This supported the Committee Managing Directors in its
role in /24, 25, 26/:

- setting the direction and strategy of the companies;

- growing and shaping the companies portfolio of
  investments and resources;

- enhancing the performance of companies assets;

- acting as custodian of the companies reputation,
  policies, and processes; and

- providing internal and external communication

Apart from supporting the work of the Committee
Managing Directors, the Corporate Centre assisted the
companies in managing their financial, tax, and corporate affairs. The Corporate Centre represented the other
organizations. The Corporate Centre comprised many
directorates depend from the activities:

- Corporate Advice (supporting each of the Managing Directors in their regional roles as well as responsibility for IT, security, contracting and procurement)
- Group Treasurer
- Group Controller
- Human Resources
- Legal

In addition to these directorates, the Corporate Centre also included the Head of Group Taxation, the Chief Information Officer, the Head of Intellectual Property, the Head of Contracting and Procurement, the Head of Group Security, the Head of Learning, and the Secretary to the Committee Managing Directors.

- **Professional Services**

These units should provide a functional support for the operating companies and service companies within the INOC. The services provided included /24, 25, 26/:

- Finance (e.g., treasury services, accounting, tax advice)

- HR (e.g., recruitment, training)

- Legal

- Intellectual property (intellectual property protection, licensing)

- Contracting and procurement

- INOC security (security advice)

- INOC aircrafts and transport

- Office services (e.g., accommodation, personnel services)

- Health (medical services, environmental and occupational health advice)

Each Professional Services unit is headed by the relevant director from the Corporate Centre.

- **The Operating Companies**

In the new organizational structure, the operating companies retained their role as the primary business entities within the INOC. Each operating company should be managed by a Board of Directors and a Chief Executive. The Chief Executive of an operating company is responsible to his/her Board and to his/her Business Director for the effective management of the operating company. The Chief Executive's responsibilities included the following /24, 25, 26, 27/:

- setting the company's strategic aims against the backdrop of any guidelines established by the Business Committee;
- providing leadership to put the strategic aims into effect and instil an entrepreneurial
- company culture;
- setting internal financial and operating targets and overseeing their achievement;
- supervising the management of the business and setting priorities;
- effective reporting on the company's activities and results to the INOC operating units

In the context of the INOC organizational structure, operating unit refers to the activities in one of the INOC Businesses which are operated as a single economic entity. An operating unit can coincide with an operating company, be a part of an operating company or straddle part or all of several operating companies. Thus, where an operating company is in one business only, the operating company is the relevant operating unit.

Changing of Culture and Behavior

A change to the existing organizational structure is only one dimension of the organizational changes of this period. If Iraq oil ministry is to improve its operational and financial performance and improve its responsiveness to the multitude of external forces that impacted its many businesses, then change needed to go beyond formal structures. The criticisms levelled at ministry of oil for being bureaucratic, inward looking, slow, and unresponsive is not about organizational structure, they are about behaviour and attitudes of the ministry and inspection body (the general inspector office). In any organizational change, a new structure may provide the right context, but ultimately it is the effects on individual and group behaviour that are critical.

It is important to mention personality test for all managers, a widely-used management tool that classifies people according to 16 psychological types. The results are people who make decisions based on logic and objective analysis and the rest are on the opposite scale. They are "feelers" who make decisions based on values and subjective evaluation.

Cost Cutting and Restructuring

The most evident short-tem impact of the reorganization is a substantial reduction in service and operational company's staffs. Savings in procurement costs and a priority for the INOC is the rationalization of capacity and reductions in operating costs in the downstream business. To facilitate this, INOC need as mentioned above embarked upon a joint Ventures:

- The amalgamation and merging of the INOC with oil majors worldwide
- Restructuring of the INOC with other businesses like chemicals business

Proposed Sketch of the existing and New Organization and Structure of Iraqi Oil Industry

- **Iraq Federal Oil Ministry**

The Iraqi Federal Oil Ministry should be charged with the overall responsibility for formulating and implementing federal government policies for the regulatory, monitoring and controlling functions of the government role in the oil industry.

- **Directorial of Oil Regulation**

The Directorial of Oil Regulation is a self-accountable body under the Federal Oil Ministry, responsible for the regulatory, monitoring and controlling functions of the upstream sector of the petroleum industry.

- **Directorial of Iraqi Petroleum Investment**

The Directorial of Iraqi Petroleum Investment should include direct business participation of the federal government for maximum economic benefit in the industry. The Minister President should create a monitoring and controlling body to prevent it from coming into conflict with its business interests in the industry. The lack of such a body explains why the government's operational efficiency and transparency are not the best.

Restructuring and reorganization of the Oil Ministry and state-owned oil companies into viable business units under the existing directorates are operatives for its commercialization and privatization counterpart:

Oil and Gas Exploration and Production Directorate Proposed Business Units:

- **Iraqi National Oil Company**
  - Exploration Company
  - South Oil Company
  - North Oil Company
  - Misan Oil Company
  - Middle Oil Company
  - Drilling Company
  - Other Oil Service Companies are possible
  - Logging Company
  - Cement and Mud Services Company
  - Other oil companies per region and or provinces are possible to consider

- **Iraq National Gas Company**
    - North Gas Filling Company
    - South Gas Filling Company
    - Middle Gas Filling Company
    - South Gas Company
    - North Gas Company
    - Other Company is possible
        - National LNG Company
    - Other gas companies per region and or provinces are possible to consider

Refineries and Petrochemical Proposed Business Units

- Petrochemical Companies
- Refineries Companies
    - South Refineries
    - North Refineries
    - Middle Refineries
    - West Refineries

Engineering and Technical Service Directorate Proposed Business Unit

- Engineering and Technical Company

- Petroleum Research and Development Company

- Information Technology Management Services

Commercial and Investment Directorate Proposed Business Units

- Oil and Gas Pipeline Company

- Oil and Gas Products Distribution Company

- Oil and Gas Products Marketing Company

- Petroleum Marketing Company

Corporate Services Directorate Proposed Business Units

- Medical and Clinical Service Company

- Estate Service Company

- Corporate Transport Service Company

Recommended Additional Business Units

- Petroleum Investment Management Companies
- Petroleum Research and Development Company
- Information Technologies Management Services
- Petroleum Products Marketing Company
- Medical and Clinical Services Company
- Estate Services Company
- Corporate Transport Services Company
- Petroleum Associated Services Management Company

- **Restructuring and Re-organisation the Oil Products Distribution in the following Companies:**

Dividing the company in many companies according to the type of products and the level of impotents:

- **Petroleum Products Marketing Company**

Receives refined petroleum products from Oil Products Distribution Company at the depots and petrochemical products from the refineries and plants and delivers same to international Marketers of these products. Supplies of crude are to the refineries through the INOC. These arrangements which make economic sense would ease petroleum products distribution in the international markets.

- **Restructuring and Re-organization of SCOP**

Dividing the activities (oil facilities, gas facilities, pipe-lines, and storages) per departments and regions.

- **Restructuring and Re-organization of Iraq Drilling Company**

  - Restructuring and Re-organisation of Iraq Drilling Company (IDC)
  - Restructuring the Iraqi Drilling Company in:
    - South Drilling Company
    - North Drilling Company
    - Middle Drilling Company
  - Create the Oil Service Companies:
    - Mud and Fluids
    - Cementing
    - Wire-Logging
    - Instruments and Tools

- **Investments in different international associated service companies**

  - Cementing Company

  - Instrument and Tools Company

  - Drilling Chemical Products

  - Mud Engineering Company

  - Well Logging Company

  - Drilling and Workover Company

  - Testing and Production Company

  - Camping and Facilities Company

- **Restructuring the Pipelines and Storages Company**

- **Restructuring the Marketing Company**

- **Restructuring and Re-organisation the Ministry of Oil as a Policy Maker**

Examples from Regional Own State Oil Companies

The following organizational charts illustrate examples of the structures of comparable oil companies in the Middle Eastern region:

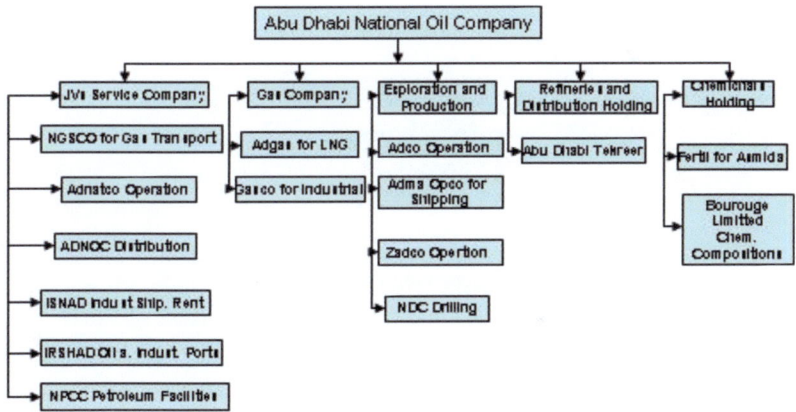

Figure 1: Draft of the organizational structure of Abu Dhabi National Oil Company (ADNOC) /28/

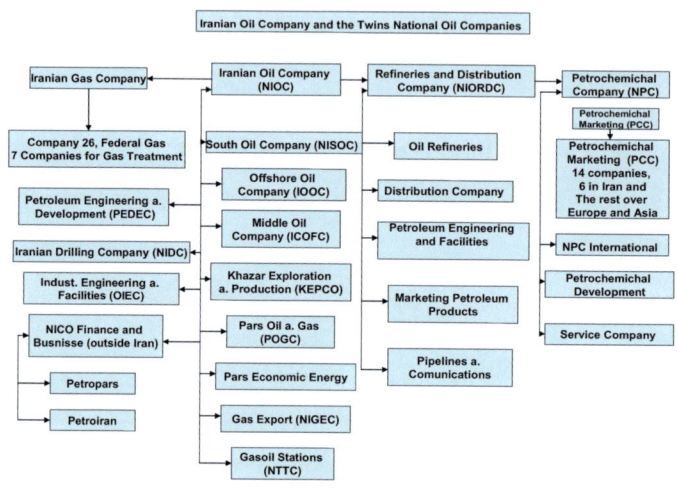

Figure 2: Draft of the organizational structure of Iranian Oil Company
and Twins National Gas Oil Companies /29/

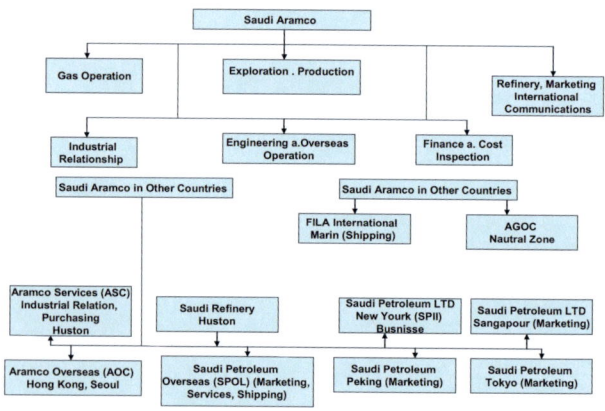

Figure 3: Draft of the organizational structure of Saudi
Aramco /30/

78

Conclusion

New oil and gas companies and departments require extensive general guidelines in Iraqi government oil and gas policy. Broad and general plans need to be condensed and refined into a more practical and concrete legal and institutional foundation in order to effectively convert the Oil and Gas industry as envisioned by the policy.

In this regard, the federal government should call for a constitutional reform the oil and gas sector. The creation of an oil and gas implementation committee would be carried out by a senior adviser nominated by the prime minister.

The existing oil and gas act is old document that was designed during the industry's infancy. It was taken in part from the scattered INOC Act and, despite the various amendments, is an outdated piece of legislation that is out of tune with contemporary global business realities. In addition, inherit laws of war are contained in several pieces of legislation. This is coupled with the fact that the numerous amendments, policy statements and regulations are dispersed in several documents and are often difficult to locate. And after the dissolution of the

INOC, it becomes a new system of regulation, which is very basic and slow compared to the international state-owned companies.

The crux of the new policy, however, revolves around the need to ensure separation and clarity of roles between the different public agencies operating in the industry. Of equally significant concern is the need to infuse strict commercial orientation in all the relevant aspects of the industry. The overall objective is to reposition the oil and gas industry in light of contemporary challenges within the sector both globally and in the domestic sphere. This is widely viewed as the best way to ensure maximum positive and sustainable impact for the Iraqi people.

The transformation of existing companies will, therefore, have to be fully commercialized, capitalized and profit-driven in keeping with international practices. In the context of the operating companies, they will operate along the entire supply chain in an integrated fashion within and outside the border of Iraq. It is therefore necessary that new structures and sub-structures of the INOC should be predominantly profit-oriented with very minimal cost sub-centers. All structures/sub-structures should commercially justify their creation. Accordingly, so will the new NOC, like most successful IOCs/NOCs in the aforementioned areas.

The Oil Assets Management Agency is indented to undertake the cost/commercial regulation of the industry, with aim of ensuring that the maximum value is derived from its oil and gas resources. It will also be accountable for the costs of oil and gas exploration and production in Iraq; and ensure that all costs, depreciation, incentives, and other allowances/benefits accorded to operators in the oil and gas sector are fully justified and lin-ine with global best practices. In so doing, the agency ensures the effective cost monitoring of Joint Venture, PSC operations and any other upstream oil and gas operations that attract Government Royalty.

A National Frontier Exploration Services should be created to regulate and stimulate petroleum exploration activities in the unassigned frontier acreages of Iraq.

The Oil Fund Board shall be responsible for determining the method by which net surplus revenue should be collected from marketing companies and recovering such net surplus revenues from the sale of oil products from marketing companies.

There is a need for an institution devoted solely to the initiation, formulation, coordination and monitoring of the implementation of policies of the oil and gas sector.

It is important to design such a framework to clearly define the mandate and powers of the regulator which would include assuming the power to make and enforce regulations; limiting the role of Government, its agencies and officials to issuing only broad, general policy guidelines to the regulator as opposed to specific directives which amount to interference with the powers of the regulator.

The tenure of executive management is guaranteed and fixed. Its abridgement is made only viable for coherent and verifiable reasons. The funding regime is structured to ensure its independence with budgetary appropriations subject to legislative oversight and not attached to ministerial budgetary provisions, i.e. with no provisions for government grants.

The establishing law provides for administrative and enforcing instruments and also makes provisions for rule-making, regulation formulation and enforcement. The staffing specifications, requirements and recruitments are specifically left in the hands of the regulator.

With regards to liberalization in the downstream sector, the need for effective regulation of the oil products supply remains. The Oil Products Distribution Company urgently needs to reorganize and restructure and requires strict separation of roles and activities in related institutions and new companies.

Real examples from the Middle Eastern Region are provided in the illustrated draft sketches in figure 1-3. These can be compared and used as a model for the future restructuring of the oil and gas industry in Iraq.

References

1. Bendell, J. and Lake, R. 2000. New Frontiers: Emerging NGO activities to strengthen transparency and accountability in business. In, Bendell, J. (ed.) Terms for Endearment. Sheffield: Greenleaf Publishing Limited, pp. 226 –238

2. Bird, F. 2004. Wealth and Poverty in the Niger Delta: Reflections on the history of Shell's Operations in Nigeria. Montreal: Concordia University

3. Department For International Development (DFID). 2005. DFID & the Private Sector: Working with the Private Sector to Eliminate Poverty, DFID, UK

4. Smith, B. (forthcoming). "Oil Wealth and Regime Survival in the Developing World, 1960-1999," American Journal of Political Science

5. Mahdavy, H. (1970). "Patterns and Problems of Economic Development in Rentier States: The Case of Iran," in M.A. Cook, Studies in the Economic History of the Middle East, Oxford University Press

6. Tealdi, L, Bruni, T.2005. Motivation and Retention of Young Workforce in the E&P Industry. IPTC 10884 presented at the International Petroleum Technology Conference held in Doha, Qatar, November 21-23

7. Harvard Business Review. January-February, p 53-62.

8. Chatterji, M. 'Training Subsidies, Technical Progress and Economic Growth', paper presented to the ESRC Development

9. This section draws from R. Cibin and R. M. Grant, "Restructuring among the world's largest oil

10. Anand, S. and Ravallion, M. 'Human Development in Poor Countries: On the Role of Private Incomes and Public majors," British Journal of Management, December 1996

11. The "Seven Sisters" were the original international oil majors

12. Carnoy, M. 'Rate of Return to Schooling in Latin America', Journal of Human Resources (1967)

13. Texaco, and Gulf. (Gulf was acquired by Chevron in 1984.)

14. C. A. J. Herkstroter, "Right for the times and right for Shell," Speech delivered in London, March 29, 1995

15. Shell Petroleum Development Company (SPDC). 2007. Shell Nigeria Annual Report 2006: People and the Environment, August 2007. Shell Petroleum Development Company, Nigeria

16. Shell Petroleum Development Company (SPDC). 2006. Shell Nigeria Annual Report 2005: People and the Environment, August 2006. Shell Petroleum Development Company, Nigeria

17. Shell Petroleum Development Company (SPDC). 2005. 2004 People and the Environment: Annual Report, May 2005. Shell Petroleum Development Company, Nigeria

18. Clark, C. 'Development Economics: The Early Years', in G.M. Meier and Dudley Seers (eds), Pioneers in Development, New York, Oxford University Press (1984)

19. Ibid. "Why is the world's most profitable company turning itself inside out?" Fortune, August 4, 1997, pp.121–5

20. Nicholson, N. 2003. How to Motivate Your Problem People. Harvard Business Review. January, p 57 - 65

21. Ibid. Reference Guide to Group Organizational Structure, Shell International Ltd, August 1996

22. Herzberg, F. 1968. One More Time: How do you motivate employees?

23. "Why is the world's most profitable company turning itself inside out?" Fortune, August 4, 1997, pp. 121-5

24. Stern, A. 2005. Who Won the Oil Wars: Why
    Government Wage War for Oil Rights. London:
    Collins and Brown

25. Tuodolo, O.F. 2007. Corporate Social Responsibility,
    Local Communities and TNCs in the Oil and Gas
    Sector of Nigeria. PhD Thesis (unpublished), Uni-
    versity of Liverpool, UK

26. "Shell shapes up for future," Speech by M. Moody-
    Stuart, San Francisco, September 18, 1998
    (www.shell.com)

27. Auty, R. (1993). Sustaining Development in the
    Mineral Economies: The Resource Curse Thesis.
    Routledge, London

28. Auty, R. (2001). Ed. Resource Abundance and
    Economic Development. Oxford University Press,
    Oxford

29. Beblawi, H. and G. Luciani (1987). Eds. The Rentier
    State. Croom Helm, New York

30. Chaudry, K. (1997). The Price of Wealth: Economies
    and Institutions in the Middle East. Cornell University
    Press, Ithaca, NY

31. M. Moody-Stuart, Changes in Shell's organization:
    comments to the Shell Global Leadership Confer-
    ence, London December 10, 1998

32. Bannon, I. and P. Collier, eds. (2003). Natural Resources and Violent Conflict: Actions and Options. World Bank

33. Collier, P. and A. Hoeffler (1998). "On Economic Causes of Civil War," Oxford Economic Papers 50, 563-573

34. Gary, I. and T. Karl (2003). Bottom of the Barrel: Africa's Oil Boom and the Poor. Catholic Relief Services, Baltimore, Maryland.

35. Marten van den Bergh; "Strengthening the Portfolio," Shell Press Release, April 3, 2000

36. Gedicks, Al (2001). Resource Rebels: Native Challenges to Mining and Oil Corporations. South End Press, Cambridge, Massachusetts

37. Gelb, A. (1988). Oil Windfalls: Blessing or Curse?" Oxford, Oxford University Press

38. Glyfason, T. (2001). "Natural Resources, Education and Economic Development," European Economic Review, Vol. 45, Nos. 4-6, pp. 847-859

39. Services', Journal of Economic Perspectives, vol.7, no.1, Winter (1993) pp 133–150

40. Behrman, J. and Birdsall, S. 'The Quality of Schooling: Quantity Alone is Misleading', American Economic Review, vol.73 (1983)

41. Human Rights Watch. (1999). The Price of Oil: Corporate Responsibility and Human Rights Violations in Nigeria's Oil Producing Communities

42. www.hrw.org/advocacy/corporations/index.htm

43. Karl, T. (1997). The Paradox of Plenty: Oil Booms and Petro-States. University of California Press, Berkeley, California

44. Karl, T. (1999), "The Perils of Petroleum: Reflections on The Paradox of Plenty," in Fueling the 21st Century: The New Political Economy of Energy, special edition of The Journal of International Affairs, vol. 53, no. 1

45. Iraq Oil Ministry Reports

46. Muhammed Abed Mazeel, "Iraq Constitution: Petroleum Resources Legislation and International Policy", disserta Verlag 2010

The author

M. Abed Mazeel (m.mazeel@hotmail.de) has been employed in many European oil companies as a senior reservoir/petroleum engineer. He has also worked as director general of Iraqi Drilling Company and director general for Oil Products Distribution Co. He was an oil industry adviser to Iraqi Prime Minister Ibrahim Al-Jaafari. M. A. Mazeel studied at the Faculty of Mining and Geology-Department of Petroleum Engineering of the University of Belgrade (Master in engineering), the Escuela Superior de Minas in Madrid (credit in applied geophysics engineering) and the University of Clausthal-Zellerfeld in Germany. He holds a PhD in petroleum engineering by the Technical University of Clausthal and is currently working on a PhD in petroleum economics. He is currently working as Subsurface Director at International Oil Company. His next books cover topics such as Gas Production Engineering and Iraq Fiscal Regimes.